LIVING AND NON-LIVING

Desert

Cassie Mayer

Heinemann
LIBRARY

www.heinemann.co.uk/library
Visit our website to find out more information about Heinemann Library books.

To order:
☎ Phone 44 (0) 1865 888066
🖹 Send a fax to 44 (0) 1865 314091
🖥 Visit the Heinemann Bookshop at www.heinemann.co.uk/library to browse our catalogue and order online.

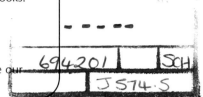

First published in Great Britain by Heinemann Library,
Halley Court, Jordan Hill, Oxford OX2 8EJ, part of Harcourt
Education. Heinemann is a registered trademark of Harcourt
Education Ltd.

Editorial: Cassie Mayer and Diyan Leake
Design: Kimberly Miracle
Illustration: Mark Beech
Picture research: Erica Martin and Melissa Allison
Production: Duncan Gilbert

Originated by Modern Age
Printed and bound in China by South China
Printing Co. Ltd

ISBN 978 0 431 18462 3
12 11 10 09 08
10 9 8 7 6 5 4 3 2 1

British Library Cataloguing in Publication Data
Mayer, Cassie
  Living and Non-living: Desert

A full catalogue record for this book is available from the
British Library.

Acknowledgements
The publishers would like to thank the following for permission
to reproduce photographs: Art Directors pp. **4**, **9**, **17**, **23**
(desert image); Corbis p. **21**, **back cover** (altrendo nature);
Digital Vision p. **18**; Getty Images pp. **5** (Walter Bibikow), **10**
(altrendo nature), **11** (Iconica/Kyle Newton), **12** (Stone/Randy
Wells), **13** (Riser/Darrell Gulin), **14** (Photographer's Choice/
Andreas Stirnberg), **23** (cactus: Stone/Randy Wells; habitat
image: Walter Bibikow); Lonely Planet pp. **15**, **16** (Carol
Polich); NHPA p. **6** (Rod Planck); Natural Born Hikers p. **8** (Cyd
Read); Nature Picture Library pp. **7** (John Cancalosi), **19** (Barry
Mansell), **22** (Gavin Hellier); Photolibrary p. **20** (OSF).

Cover photograph of bush sunflowers and yucca in the
California desert reproduced with permission of Getty Images/
Taxi (Ron and Patty Thomas).

Contents

A desert habitat

A desert is an area of land.
A desert is hot and dry.

A desert has living things.
A desert has non-living things.

Lizard

black collared lizard

Is a lizard a living thing?

Does a lizard need food? *Yes*.
Does a lizard need water? *Yes*.

Does a lizard need air? *Yes.*

Does a lizard grow? *Yes.*

So a lizard is a living thing.

Cactus

Is a cactus a living thing?

Sunshine makes plant food.

Does a cactus need food? *Yes.*
Does a cactus need water? *Yes.*

11

Does a cactus need air? *Yes.*

Does a cactus grow? *Yes.*

So a cactus is a living thing.

Rock

Is a rock a living thing?

Does a rock need food? *No.*
Does a rock need water? *No.*

Does a rock need air? *No*.

Does a rock grow? *No*.

So a rock is not a living thing.

Scorpion

Is a scorpion a living thing?

centipede

Does a scorpion need food? *Yes.*
Does a scorpion need water? *Yes.*

Does a scorpion need air? *Yes.*

Does a scorpion grow? *Yes.*

So a scorpion is a living thing.

A desert is home to many things.

A desert is an important habitat.

Picture glossary

 **cactus** a plant that grows in the desert

 **desert** a habitat that is hot and dry in the day. Deserts can be cold at night.

 **habitat** area where plants and animals live

Index

Notes for Parents and Teachers
Before reading
Talk about what living things need – food, water, and air. Talk about things that move but which are not living – cars, boats, planes. How do they move?

After reading
Give one child a picture such as a boat, tree, or baby. The child must not show the picture to the rest of the class. Encourage the other children to ask questions to guess what the picture shows. First they must determine if the thing is living or non-living (needs food, water, and air, and it grows). Then they can ask other questions: Does it move? Does it travel on land? Is there one in the classroom?

Talk about how babies grow, from lying on its back to rolling on to its tummy, siting up, crawling, toddling, walking, andrunning. Ask the children to do each of the actions of the "growing" story.